Shorts ...
Tailored For Kids

To: Cali -
Happy reading! Good Luck in all of
your adventures!

Cheryl L VanWinkle
2010

Shorts ... Tailored For Kids

Cheryl VanWinkle

Library of Congress Control Number: 2010914194
ISBN: Hardcover   978-1-4535-8442-2
               Softcover   978-1-4535-8441-5
               Ebook   978-1-4535-8443-9

This book was printed in the United States of America.

To order additional copies of this book, contact:
Xlibris Corporation
1-888-795-4274
www.Xlibris.com
Orders@Xlibris.com
81448

Contents

ABC's 9

Yo-Ho-Ho 13

The Handprint Magician 17

Princess 21

Good Morning 25

Bubbles 29

Firefly, Firefly 33

Ants In My Pants 37

Circus 41

Pretty Purple Barrette 45

Jellyfish 49

Sandbox Grit 53

What's In Your Backyard? 57

3 Little Birdies 61

Spaghetti Night—What A Mess 65

Glow Tails 69

Happy Birthday Day 73

Fireworks 77

This children's book was inspired by my son, Logan who helped me to tap into my creative side. Thanks is also extended to my husband, Shawn for his support and agreeing to be the illustrator, my friends and family who have been encouraging through this process and finally to Dr. James Schreiber, for without his compassion, dedication and expertise we may never have had our dreams of parenthood come true. To everyone, thank you.

ABC's

A is for apple,
B is for boy,
C is for cat that jumps for his toy.
D is for dog who chases the cat,
E is for everyone who watches and claps.
F is for friend who is there when you're sad,
G is for gifts that make you happy and glad.
H is for honey, watch out! There's bees!
I is for itchy when ants crawl up your knees.
J is for jokes, laughing keeps you well,
K is for kite, flying high as a church bell.
L is for love, it's what your family feels,
M is for monkeys throwing banana peels!
N is for nature, where you see the animals and trees,
O is for octopus with eight arms that squeeze!
P is for picture—which can say more than words,
Q is for quiet when you don't want to be heard . . . Sshh.
R is for running as fast as you can,
S is for snowflakes falling gently in your hand.
T is for turtle that walks on the ground,
U is for ukulele, that plays a beautiful sound.
V is for vegetables, vase and violin,
W is for the wishing well you throw your pennies in.
X is for eXtraordinary, and that is what YOU are!
Y is for yak, yo-yo, yawn and yarn.
Last but not least we have the letter Z.
The 26th letter in the alphabet you see.
Beginning words such as zany,zip,zipper and zoom,
There are many letters in the alphabet, it's true.

What Would You Draw?

Yo-Ho-Ho

Arrgh, Matey!
Where have you been?
It's time to set foot on this precious gem.

The boat is eager to sail through cold waters.
Please, don't make her wait any longer!

Grab your boots and put on your hat.
Fasten your sword, you're gonna need that.

We will sail the seas of blue,
And hunt for treasures, too!

Crashing through the waves,
We will chase the sea monsters away.

So, c'mon, let's go!
You are moving much too slow.

Our Captain is you, Yo-Ho-Ho!

What Would You Draw?

The Handprint Magician

Little tiny handprints all around.
On the table, the couch, even the ground.

Pressed against the windowpane,
They must have been watching the falling rain.

Who do these little handprints belong to?
I wonder, I wonder, I wonder who.

Tiny handprints on the door.
Tiny handprints on the floor.
Where next will these handprints explore?

What is that I see?
There are now tiny handprints on my knee!

Up the stairs and through the door,
I spied a little boy on the floor.
Covered in dirt, covered in grime,
He said "Mommy, please get off the slime".

The tub filled with bubbles as he plopped in.
My little handprint magician is squeaky clean again!

What Would You Draw?

Princess

Big, white, fluffy clouds way up high.
What lies beyond?
Is there a castle in the sky?

A big castle glowing bright,
With magical unicorns and fairies in flight.
Surely this is a princess's delight.

Clouds to bounce on, a cloud for my bed.
Nothing is softer for a princess's tired head.

Sliding down rainbows made of reds, yellows, greens and blues.
Landing in magical watery pools. Splash!

Dressed in pretty dresses and shoes
A robe and a crown and even sparkly jewels.

For this is a princess's castle and I am a princess, you see.
Playing, dancing and singing happily.

What Would You Draw?

Good Morning

Good Morning, Good Morning, Good Morning,
I love you, I love you, I love you.

What did you dream of while you were asleep?
Running in the tall green grass?
Throwing a football pass?
Flying as high as the birds you see?
Chasing away the rabbits, the squirrels and the bees?

Well today is a new day and there is much to do.
Many adventures lay ahead of you.

So, let's get ready and welcome the day.
Let's get ready so we can go play!

Hurry, before the sun sets and the sky grows dark.
Hurry, and play before bedtime embarks.

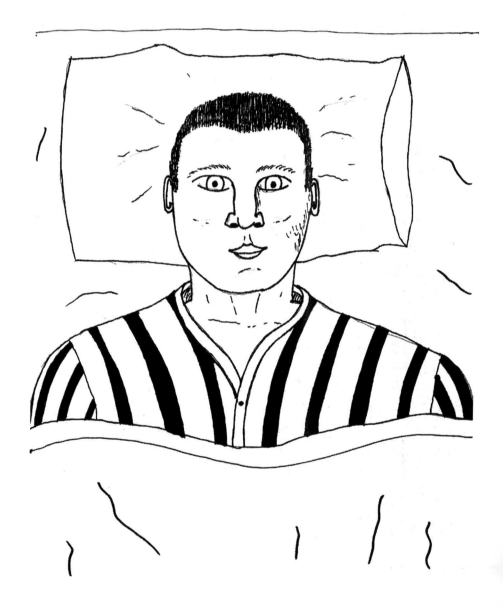

What Would You Draw?

Bubbles

Bubbles, bubbles in the air
Bubbles, bubbles everywhere

Bubbles floating all around
Bubbles floating up and down

Floating over the grass below
Floating over the sea and snow

Floating up through the trees
Floating even when you sneeze!

Where oh where do these bubbles go?
Where oh where will they blow?

What Would You Draw?

Firefly, Firefly

Firefly, firefly you shine so bright,
Just like the moon in the dark, dark night.

You twinkle here, you twinkle there.
I have so much fun chasing you everywhere!

Upwards, downwards, round and round,
I get so dizzy I fall to the ground!

Firefly, firefly you shine so bright,
Just like the moon in the dark, dark night.

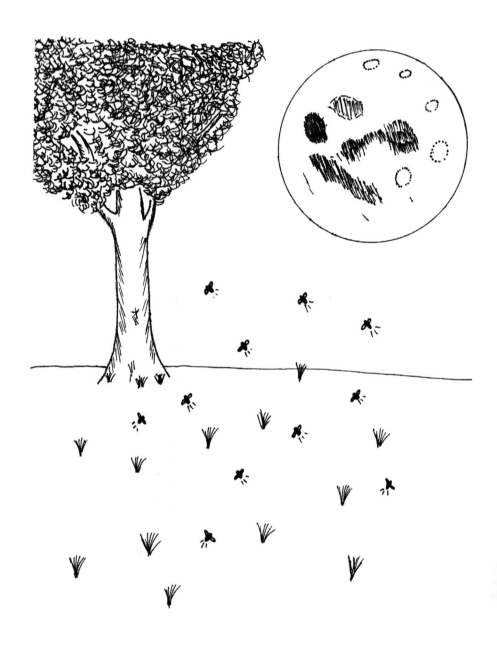

What Would You Draw?

Ants In My Pants

Ants, ants in my pants.
Making me itch, making me dance.

Oh how did these ants get in my pants?

What Would You Draw?

Circus

Hey, hey, what do you know,
We are going to see a circus show!

I'm so excited, I've never been.
Can't you see my smiling grin?

What will we see at this circus show?

Cotton Candy blowers,
Fearless flame throwers,
Trampoline jumpers,
Enormous snake tamers.

Big tall elephants to ride on,
Bike riding bears with tutus on.
Tigers with an echoing roar,
Trapeze artists who are able to soar!
Face painters painting faces,
Clown jugglers juggling vases!

Oh my gosh it sounds like fun.
We better hurry, we better run.
We don't want to miss the show.
So, come on everybody, let's go!

What Would You Draw?

Pretty Purple Barrette

I have a purple barrette, placed gently in my hair.
My pretty barrette goes with me almost everywhere.

Keeping my hair out of my eyes, there's so much to
see . . .
What a great surprise!

Adorned with butterflies and sparkles, too
My purple barrette matches my dress and my shoes.

Oh how pretty my barrette makes me feel,
Now to go find my mommy's heels!

What Would You Draw?

Jellyfish

I am swimming with the fish,
A giant sea of jellyfish.

Looking soft and squishy,
Bobbing in the water nice and gently.

They don't talk,
They don't make a sound.
Not a peep from any around.

Floating as quiet as can be.
Bobbing up and down peacefully.

The jellyfish and me.

What Would You Draw?

Sandbox Grit

Gritty sand in my toes,
Gritty sand up my nose.

Gritty sand in my eyes and hair.
Oh my gosh, it's everywhere!

Oh my gosh, oh my geez,
I have sand up to my knees!

Where oh where does the sand end?
What do you expect when it's a sandbox you're in?

What Would You Draw?

What's In Your Backyard?

What's in your backyard?
What's in my backyard?

Let's go explore!

There's . . . .
Green grass to tickle your toes,
Flowers that'll tickle your nose.
Birds that fly high in the sky,
Rabbits that hop on by.
Crickets that jump and chirp,
Beetles that dig in the dirt.
Slugs that are slimy and squishy,
Worms that are long and icky . . . Eeewwww!
Squirrels chasing each other up the trees,
Bzzz, Bzzz sounds the bee.
Butterflies floating with the breeze,
Yucky pollen that can make you sneeze. Achoo!
Little ants working as a team,
Snakes that slither and make me SCREAM!
Eight-legged spiders catching their food,
Uh-oh, watch out for animal poo!

What Would You Draw?

3 Little Birdies

Three little birdies flying so high,
Through the wind up, up in the sky.

Their wings grew tired,
Their mouths dry.
Whew! How much work it is to fly.

Three little birdies spied a tiny boat,
And sat with the fisherman on his heavy wool cloak.

The fisherman said," Well my friends, you look a wee tired,
Take a rest here while I catch some dinner.

The three little birdies feasted away.
Then stood up, said "Thank you, sir, have a nice day"!
And the three little birdies flew far, far away.

What Would You Draw?

Spaghetti Night—What A Mess

I like spaghetti,
I like meatballs.
I really like making a mess with tomato sauce!

Sauce in my eyes,
Sauce in my hair,
Sauce way up in the air!

Down the front of me,
And even on my pants.

How did I get sauce in my underpants?

What Would You Draw?

Glow Tails

Fireflies, fireflies all around.
Fireflies, fireflies floating up from the ground.
With tails all aglow,
They put on quite a show!
Twinkling here, twinkling there,
I love to chase them everywhere!

What Would You Draw?

Happy Birthday Day

Hip Hip Hooray!
Today is a birthday day!
Whose birthday is it? I'm not sure.
Is it mine?
It is yours?
Is it the lady over there wearing pearls?
Is it the zebra's at the zoo?
Could even be the giraffe's, the addax or even the
ladybug's, too.

Whose birthday is it? Whose, whose, whose?
Whose ever birthday day it is, I'm sure it'll be fun.
Playing outside in the warm, bright sun.
Running with all sorts of balloons,
Eating cake and ice cream, too.
Laughing at the joke telling clowns,
Oh no, there will not be any, not one, single frown.

So hip hip hooray!
Another smile is to be made for it is someone's birthday
day.
Happy Birthday Day! Yeah!!!

What Would You Draw?

Fireworks

Blast! Bam! Boom!
Zip, Zip, Zoom!

What is that I hear?
Is it near?

Who could be making such a ruckus at this time?
Doesn't everyone know it is past my bedtime?

Whatever or whomever it is, it sure sounds fun!

Maybe I'll take a peek,
Maybe I'll take a sneak.
To find what it is that is keeping me from my sleep.

Oh wow, oh my, look what I spy.
Out my window the sky is bright.
With sparkly reds, twinkly greens and glittery whites!

What is that you say?
This is a fireworks display?

Oh yippee! Oh yay!
Can I stay . . . .
Up for the show to see the twinkling glow?

Just a few more minutes until the party is done.
Just a few more minutes to have some more fun.

Sparkle, sparkle, swirl, swirl,
Zip, zoom . . . BOOM!

Now the show has reached it's end,
It is now time for me to crawl into bed.

The End.

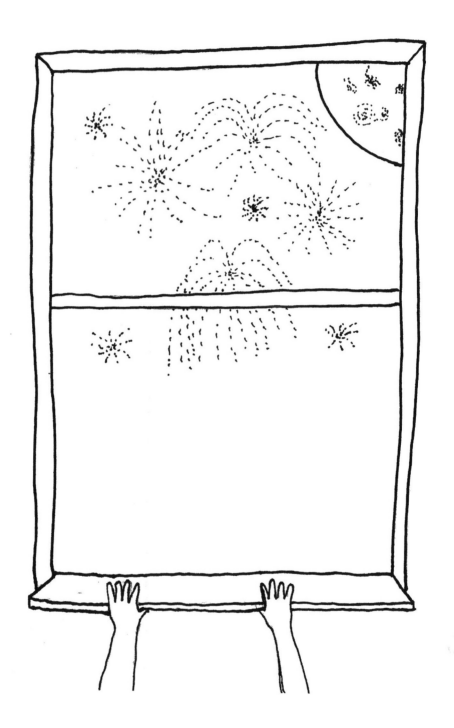

What Would You Draw?